A
S
NO
CREATIVE
ESCAPOLOGY

© **GOLDEN RULE PUBLICATIONS**
The publisher makes no representation, express or implied, with regard to the accuracy of the information contained in this book and cannot accept any legal responsibility for any errors or omissions that may take place.

Art Director

John Clement

Series Editor

Alex Woodcock- Clarke

Printed and bound by Whitstable Litho, Millstrood Road,

Whitstable, Kent.

ISBN 1 899299 25 4

First published in Great Britain in 1994 by Golden Rule Publications, Eldon Lodge, 52 Victoria Road, London W8 5RQ.

Tel 071-937 3324. Fax 071-937 1137

THE ART OF SAYING NO

CREATIVE ESCAPOLOGY

by
A.B. Crombie

HOW TO SAY NO

Oh it's hard to say Onimackata lookat cheecheechee
But in Tonga that means no
If I ever have the money
'Tis to Tonga I shall go
For every lovely lady there
Will gladly make a date
And by the time she's said Onimackata
lookat choochoochoo
It is usually too late
(Flanders & Swan)

The N Word

Saying no is something that none of us is very good at. Let's face it we don't get a lot of practice because it is usually much more exciting and pleasurable to say "Yes" or even "Yes please" or even "Yes, yes, yes, yes.... Oh noooooo. Dammit, why didn't you think about cricket scores like a real man? Or Ian Hislop?"

Ideally, saying no must be done elegantly and specifically, with the lifting of an eyebrow, an enigmatic half-smile and a flutter of the lashes. If you are a woman, this will leave the impression that you are saying "No... but maybe"; if you are a man, the impression is more likely to be that you are a vicar defrocked because you couldn't keep your hands off the treble section or else are in the early, twitching stages of Parkinsons. Improvise.

In either case, if you are not careful, you could be blocking an avenue that might one day be a something you want to investigate. So always be aware very of to what and whom you are saying no - and then offer a positive alternative. Who knows?, the old bat, stinking of cheap gin and Embassy Regal who accosts you in Piccadilly for the price of a Yankee on Derby Day could always turn out to be the Queen Mother. (In this case, saying no translates into: "Your Majesty, I beg to announce I don't have a nicker on me, absolutely stony. But Her Royal Highness, the Princess Royal is always good for a pony").

And so to the Golden Rules of saying NO

Disclaimer

Before we start, a little word of warning - all the advice in this book should be ignored.

The author was not able to say no to writing it, and the publisher could not say NO to publishing it either. And you couldn't say NO to buying it. Someone, somewhere along the line, is showing a regrettable lack of discipline. This line of mugs wouldn't disgrace the shelves of a Methodist soup kitchen. On the other hand, this is exactly the same principle that's kept Jeffery Archer alive and well and living in luxury all these years, so who's complaining?

The Basics

If you can help it in any way, don't say no.

Say "Maybe" or "Perhaps' or "Possibly" or "In the not too distant future" or "Once in a Blue Moon" or "During the next Labour administration" or "When Kampuchea takes her rightful place in the comity of nations" or "When Boeing can design a condom which can take all of me/you". "Not on your Nelly" always begs the question - "Who's Nelly"

The Definite and the Final NO

Try to make your NO definite, but not necessarily final.

This is the difference:

The definite NO is accompanied by a lingering half-caress of the other person's cheek suggestive of a regretful, even tragic yearning that must be denied, at least today.

The final NO is accompanied by a clip across the

chops that sets the dentures rattling like a flamenco played at 45 rpm.

The Cost of Saying NO

Saying NO is not difficult but think of the cost. It can be the cheapest possible alternative, but then again, you've lost so much potential.

Decca turned down the Beatles. George Raft turned down "Casablanca". And John F. Kennedy turned down the Lincoln Continental Classic (the one that doesn't come with the easy to operate roll-down, enjoy-the-sunshine, look-isn't-that-the-book-depository soft-top as standard).

On the other hand Rupert Murdoch said; "The Hitler Diaries? I'll take as many as you can churn out. We can sort out later why the Fuhrer wrote on K-Mart headed stationery".

SAYING NO AROUND THE WORLD

In English

First of all it is important to know how to say no in more than one language.

NO in English is easy, we all know that one. It is the same in American though you have to put a bit of a nasal whine into the O part. If you want to be polite about it and frightfully English, you should really put "I am so sorry but" in front of any NO that you are about to commit. It prepares the ground, and the recipient of the N word will be expecting what is to follow, but there is no need to be quite that gracious.

The English have developed a form of politeness verging on fear, which asks a question almost begging the answer NO. Going into a hostelry at 7 o'clock in the evening, an Englishman will approach the lady behind the bar with trepidation and diffidently enquire: "I'm sorry, are you serving food yet?"

To which she will reply: "No, the kitchen doesn't open until 7.15."

And, all too aware of his lack of social nouse, he will slink away to an obscure table and nurse a pint of warm beer until the management deigns to accept his money.

No other country in the world behaves quite like this.

In some circumstances the Englishman finds it nearly as difficult to say NO as the Japanese, who would rather subject himself to ritual evisceration that utter the word.

The Englishman will be sitting in a doctor's waiting room riddled with hives, piles, terminal this and that and a full colostomy bag and when an aquaintance asks him "Are you well?" he'll reply something along the lines of: "Very fit thanks, mustn't grumble. You?"

The well brought up Englishwoman also has trouble with the N word under certain social circumstances. Being asked to dance at a formal-ish party for instance. She feels it would be breaching social etiquette to reply: "To be perfectly honest, I'd far rather be married to a Gloucester builder" or "In your dreams, Buster", so she dances and is marked for the rest of the evening with the sweaty hand mark in the small of the back.

NO, incidentally, doesn't need to be spoken. It can also be expressed by a vigorous shake of the head (but not too early in the morning or after dinner when it is possible that you have consumed too much alcohol - it can have disastrous effects on your internal system - i.e. volcanic). It is worth knowing, though that a vigorous shake of the head means Yes in India and a large swathe of the South East Asian subcontinent.

NO In Europe

NO in most European Countries, and in South

America, is Non which is pronounced as though it were a large and sweating pig saying NO - which it mostly is.

However, in Greece and Middle European countries, if you raise your eyebrows roll up your eyes and tut your refusal will be understood - either that or they will think that you are completely mad, and you can get away with anything after that

Beware though of Ne (as if it were a goat saying NO), because this actually means yes. Similarly, saying Ne to a goat.

NO On The Fringes of Europe

In Spain they have got it down to a 'T'. Spanish administrators are always reluctant to say no, but have a wonderful way of putting off the decision - the word Mañana comes into play. I know of one particular case where a customs official in Marbella International Airport managed to say Mañana to one poor tourist on a Club 18-30 charter so long that by the time he got out he was only good for a Saga Holiday for the active elderly.

In Ireland, Mañana also means NO - but without quite the same sense of urgency.

Ne and Nikoli are the words to be used in Czeckoslovakia to any thing at all, because you won't have a clue what you were asked. The problem with the Czechs is that, like South-East Asia, the affirmative is accompanied by a vigorous shaking of the head and the negative by nodding. This can be highly confusing whether one is attempting instant seduction or merely asking directions.

To Turkish rug or opium dealers, just say Hayir. I believe this also means, "Not Guilty".

NO International

Other essential words to learn on the great subject of NO are:

Nix (well Americans were never very sensible were they?)

Niet (this word will be recognised all over the ex-Soviet Union) and

Nein (for use over the rest of Middle Europe, where

the tut didn't get through but the Panzer did).

Also worth knowing is Mai Chai which means NO in Thai. This is essential if anybody asks you to carry their luggage through customs, or to any willowy, sloe-eyed charmer in a split silk skirt but with a disturbingly prominent Adams Apple who might accost you in downtown Bangkok.

NO - The French Disconnection

Beware though, of the French who occasionally break through their barriers of rudeness and instead of saying Non say Merci.

This, meaning Thankyou in English, implies the positive, but actually means the opposite. They think that they are being amazingly polite, but they are an easily offended bunch of people, so if you take them the wrong way, they will be mortally offended.

Sometimes they do say "Non" - but, for the French, this little word is charged with manifold and menacing nuance. For example, when President de Gaulle said "Non" to British requests to join the EEC in the early 1970's it meant; "Ha, ha, ha, where are your miniskirts, warm beer, Milord Harold Wilson and Bay City Rollers now, perfidious swine?" In such a case, the only diplomatic response is to withdraw murmuring the words "I'm sorry that you still haven't forgiven us for winning the war for you..." in a discreet but audible tone.

The Brits have become very lazy, linguistically, and tend to say "Thankyou" when accepting something offered, instead of "Yes, please". This is fine in England. It doesn't work in France and Spain, however, where saying "Thankyou" is understood, quite correctly, to imply "No thankyou". By the time you've seen the waiter whip your plate away a few times and watched the partner you thought you were getting on with so well disappearing with a puzzled look on his face, you'll get the hang of it.

NO In The Far East

In China it not worth getting yourself into the situation of having to make this particular statement, and the likelihood of it happening is very remote - it is still a communist country and people still seldom ask for anything because they expect the answer to be NO. Besides, they offer so little that you have nothing to refuse.

Except the food. Chinese food in China is not the same as Chinese food down Peckham High Street. It comprises chicken's feet, one thousand year old eggs and bird's nest soup made out of insect phlegm. Say NO to Chinese food in such a way that your host does not lose face. Find yourself a dose of gastric 'flu or malaria. Do not say: "I'm so sorry but as a condition of being a Blue Peter Gold Badge Holder, I have renounced Labrador in all its forms". After this kind of kind of comment you could end up as nothing more than a dirty stain beneath a tank track on Tianenmen Square.

Japan is a different story. It is possibly the most difficult of all. There is no word in Japanese that translates the word NO, in fact any circumlocution implying the negative is regarded as a mortal insult, but if you suck air in through your teeth, look very very alarmed, cock your head on one side and say [JAP CHARACTER] it usually works. If not a slightly stronger alternative is

[JAP CHARACTER] and when all else fails try [JAP CHARACTER]

After that just tell them to f*** off..

THE MEANING OF NO

Different Inflections

The different inflections used in saying NO are also extremely important; You can imply anything from "Yes please I would very much like that" or "That's the most interesting piece of gossip that I have heard in the last month" to "That is the most ghastly suggestion I have heard in my entire life" and "I absolutely refuse" to "Why don't you be a Cossack with an urgent delivery and I'll be a handy 'My Little Pony'".

You must make sure that you use these inflections to your fullest advantage. This takes practice. We suggest that you find a time when you are on your own. Then sit in front of a mirror and see how many different ways of expressing yourself with the N word you can find. An hour or two should be sufficient

Good luck.

Do be careful though, the wind might change, your face might stick and for the rest of your life you'll look like someone sucking an egg out of an invisible chicken.

But then you'll be very popular at parties.

Different Gestures

The gestures accompanying your negative also have meaning.

A firm wave means: "NO - and goodbye".

A gentle wave means "NO - but maybe later".

Slapping your head with your palm means: "NO - how could you be so stupid?"

Slapping someone else's head means; "NO - and hear that echo? It means no twice, stupid".

Raising your hands above your head and gesticulating wildly while treading saltwater means: "NO, I'm not waving but drowning".

The index finger extended and then bent means

"Never mind what I said - come here now".

The middle finger extended and moved upwards means... Well, why don't you try it on the next taxi driver who cuts you up on the Hanger Lane Gyratory Complex and see for yourself.

SAYING NO SOCIALLY.

The A List & The B List.

Divide your acquaintanceship into an A List and a B List.

Into the A List go Michelle Pfeiffer, mysterious little, old millionaires, members of the royal family of Spain, Eric Clapton, anyone with a large yacht, prospective lovers, the managers of vast, international corporations and generally, anyone rich, famous and lovely. You yourself and all of us would fit naturally into this list.

Into the B List goes Michelle from "Eastenders", mysterious little old men who loiter outside public lavatories, members of the Kray Family, Eric Bristow, anyone with a large wart, prospective CPAs, bank managers and, generally, anyone else.

These are not your type.

Always say Yes to the A list but never say NO to the B list, just postpone and rearrange where necessary. Eventually, your diary will be full, and the B list will become gradually so bored with the cancellations and postponements that they will find themselves on C and even D lists. (The D list includes Serb militia leaders, Edwina Curry and that man who takes the seat beside you on an otherwise empty bus and tells you that squirrels are the Devil's oven mitts).

Getting Out Of B List Engagements

It is easy to tell when someone for whom you do not have a great deal of time (i.e. who is either on your B or your C list) has you on their A list. You will find yourself the target of the continual invitations to different occasions, often intimate. It is essential to get yourself demoted, but as has been explained, without causing offence. You must match the continual invitation with a similarly unexciting excuse.

Do not repeat yourself too often, but make it clear

that what you will be doing instead is, though not necessarily the most exhilarating, is certainly something you would not dream of cancelling. It may take a while for the relegation, but nobody can put up with the "I'm visiting my grand mother", "I'm going out every day next week, perhaps we can meet for a drink sometime in the week after next" routine for ever.

The "I'm washing my hair tonight" excuse is not recommended. It makes the recipient think; "This person believes that a date with Head & Shoulders is more fascinating than meeting other people. What a sad person".

Also, it does tend to make them suspicious if you're bald.

Getting Out of A List Engagements

You will find a list of stock excuses in refusals to dinner

Getting out of A list engagements. The secret here is to make your excuse more exciting than the invitation you are declining - and thus generate a little envy too.

"Sorry - I'm finishing my golden rules guide to man hunting that night. And tonight is field trials".

"Sorry, the Chippendales are coming over and I'm going to French polish them".

"Sorry but it's the SAS Regimental Ball that night. I could give you details but then I'd have to spread-eagle you on the ground and shoot you in the back of the head".

Making Up A Party To Go On Holiday

It is essential to make this a really good excuse. This is partly because whoever it is that has invited you obviously likes you and thinks that you will get on with the rest of the crowd. Going off on a holiday with a bunch of other people seldom works - someone always has to be the centre of attention and another of the party invariably spends too long in the bathroom in the morning and uses up all the hot water.

Sorry, but your boss needs you to fly out to the Bahamas, Hong Kong or Australia to broker a very delicate deal (This won't necessarily work if it's known that you're only a till attendant at Bettabuys).

You've taken your holiday in cash so that you can buy a new car/ piano /sofa/ prosthetic limb/ to pay off gambling debts with the mob.

You're having an affair with someone very famous, very rich and very married and you had planned to spend this time with them in some secret location (When you give this excuse, drop enough hints to ensure that your phantom lover is not judged to be somebody too obviously down-market like a minor royal or Jim Davidson)

On the whole, it is probably better to think up some reason which will discourage anyone from wanting you to go with them on holiday at all. "Does the hotel do macrobiotic food?" Should scare your potential holiday partners enough". If not, "Sure, I want to do something a little unusual this year - how about cycling over the Middle East and seeing how many borders we can cross" might have the desired effect but if all else fails try "Yes but I only ever sunbathe in the nude, will you rub on my Eczema Preparation? It's made from real goat glands" and that should do the trick

Refusing The Weekend

Best friends, ex-lovers and brothers or sisters will always be happy if you give them a little intimate detail of your life as way of cancellation. "NO darling I can't possibly come for the weekend. I've just met this fabulous person called Luke/Lucia and we have been in bed for the last 36 hours. I can't possibly bear to be parted from him/her. Can you make dinner next Wednesday and I'll tell you all about it" should work. If it isn't true, for God's sake remember to cancel dinner on Wednesday, because you have realised what a shallow person Luke/Lucia is and you just don't want to have to talk about him/her.

This is a very good line to try on a pestering man or woman as well. In fact it is one of the great refusals of all time.

It is important that you are careful not to use this excuse too often. Your friends might begin to think you have the sexual appetite of a chimp and the discrimination of a Messalina.

You'll know when you've gone too far when you start receiving unsolicited job offers from Conservative Central Office.

NB Never try this on your parents or grand parents.

Refusing time with Parents Grandparents

The old favourites - I've got a spot, I'm too tired/I'm too depressed/I don't feel very well etc. (delete where appropriate) don't work. They've seen you in worse states. I mean, do you remember reaching puberty?

They don't think much of "I've just got to go down to the clinic" either, though why not I have never really understood.

"I've met a new man/woman" doesn't work either because you may end up with the family synod being called in to judge.

"I've too much work" is OK but then you have their

concern over your welfare, and if it isn't true, it causes such guilt that finding a better excuse is worth the trouble.

No, senior members of your immediate family deserve (well perhaps not deserve, but certainly require) something a little better. There is always something that your elders and (perhaps) betters aspire to, whether it is social or sporting.

If you say you've had a sudden invitation to the Grand National or the Cheltenham Gold Cup, Glyndebourne, Henley, Grouse Shooting or whatever they are into, it normally works a treat.

Beware, though, of Wimbledon Tennis for any of the important matches, because the crowds are normally caught on film, and, if you weren't there, you have a serious problem. You must remember that all Grandparents now have a video recorder:

"Well, darling, we recorded all of the Manchester United match and went through it frame by frame and you weren't there. It took us fifteen hours but we so wanted to see you... Oh it was

Manchester City...".

Again, be warned, many's the cosy will-reading turned that's been transformed into an emotional charnel house when a prospective legatee learns that his neglected grandparent has left everything, including the Canalettos, to the Meals On Wheels lady.

Saying NO To The Queen

In principle, accept everything the Queen gives you - you've paid for it anyway. Be careful of life peerages though and pick and choose your title carefully. You might well fancy the idea of being "Baron So and So of London" but the Honours Office reserves all the best towns and counties for senior politicians, generals, billionaires and anyone who has kept the Tory party afloat, so you could end up as Lady Such and Such of Crawley New Town.

If you really must turn down an invitation or an honour, don't do it for the prosaic reasons that other publicity seekers do so: "I cannot take this MBE while there are three million tragic unemployed...".

Yawn, yawn.

Try instead: "I'm sorry Your Majesty but as a charter member of the RSPCA, I couldn't possibly except anything from anyone who wears an electric yellow hat with an electric yellow coat to open Ascot. It frightens the horses".

While an effective method of refusing an invitation to a Garden Party you can almost certainly count on receiving another invitation by return of post, this time to the Tower.

You should always say No to Royal Garden Party invitations, though. The invitation on the mantelpiece - or prominently on the top of the wastepaper basket - is all you require. You will be unlikely to meet the Queen if you do go; you're not allowed to talk to her about anything you want to (selling fire insurance) and, when you get home and take your souvenirs out of your handbag, you'll find that all the cups and saucers you've cleverly secreted have only "J. Lyons Catering" on them to remind you of your moment in the sun.

Saying NO To A Queen

Campest excuses are best. Queens understand them

without hesitation -

"Not tonight, dearie. My body aches all over because that brute of a masseur really pummelled me this afternoon" will elicit sympathy.

Others like "That nasty little man who came over to read my meter left footprints all over my lino and I have to go home and remove all trace of him" might work

If you are seriously worried, though, just remember to keep your back to the wall.

TIMING

Saying NO from the start

Cocktail parties are social gatherings not to be missed. You never know who might be there, and what sort of useful nugget of information you might pick up. But if you get landed with some dreadful man with bottle bottom glasses, halitosis and spots who you then discover is the brother of the host, and what is worse, he asks you out, there are some great lines that you can use.

"What star sign are you?" is a good opening line to the final refusal. "Oh I have a real problem with Taureans. I know you'll hurt me. They always do".

If he then discovers that you have ended up with a Taurean any time in the future you can always say that you are bit worried but the exception proves the rule.

Other great lines of this ilk are:

"My energy isn't right"

"My aura is becoming unsettled"

"Do you believe in evil spirits?"

"Your subconscious is trying to change my otherness"

"I am Linda Blair (or Max Von Sydow). You might have seen me in "The Exorcist". Shall I do my projectile vomiting party-piece now?"

You must be careful about the people on whom you lose these lines, though. People will think you are a real nut, and it is not difficult to get a reputation for being very peculiar, and if it is a very close friend who is the host it may not wash.

NO at the last minute

Roll out all the favourite excuses but make them sound convincing (if that is the impression you actually want to give). A non-definitive list in no particular order reads:

No time
No money
No sense

No transport
Nothing to wear
Minor Flu
I've got to see my mother
I've got to wash my hair
The washing machine is broken
I've got to tidy up my sock drawer

NO (Advanced Students Only)

There are more technical ones that deeply impress the recipient of the excuse

"I've broken down, and it looks as though there is something cracked in my half shaft" sounds so extraordinary that it has to be true Only a mechanic would question whether it was possible, and whether your car ever had a half shaft to break. Or whether, in fact, you're referring to your car.

Other good ones - "My computer seems to have wiped its backup and I have to play with it until I find it in its memory" makes it sound as though you actually understand how computer programmes work, or "It is really my fault but I got the A and C drive confused in my backing up so I not only have to redo I have to re-format" will deeply impress anyone who has to use computers with the amount of work you are faced with but they may be deeply surprised by 1 - your stupidity and 2 - your dedication.

"I haven't got the blend quite right of my merlot and cabernet franc and I can't really stop until I do" will make your recipient wide eyed wide eyed with your brilliance at wine making - he needn't know that you are only making a fruit salad with peach slices in heavy syrup out of a tin.

Forgetting To Cancel - No Show.

There are few better ways to commit social suicide than forgetting to say no - walking into the Reform Club dressed as Ben Elton is one which we shall not go into in these pages

No-show is a major faux pas. I am afraid that "I put it on the wrong page in my diary", "Oh I'm sorry I forgot" or any of the excuses above are not good enough. You can only get away with this if you have had appendicitis and crashed the car on the way to hospital.

The only way of crawling back is a telegram (or tele-message depending on where it has to go to), a return invitation, a letter of apology and a bunch of flowers.

NO should never actually cost much, and you are beginning to talk about upwards of £50 here, and promotion to the A list. So make sure you said No, in the first place, OK?

If the worse comes to the worse, your excuse must involve apology, explanation and self-abasement in equal measure: something like a mumbled: "Sorry - women's problems" might be enough, redolent as it is of the complexities of bathroom plumbing and the sheer disgustingness of a James Herbert novel, but not if you're a man.

A man should have to try something along the lines of; "A little kiddie disappeared at the end of our street. The police interviewed me for five hours. Don't worry. I've got an alibi. I was with you, wasn't I?".

In either case, don't expect to be asked again.

"Not Forgetting To Cancel - No Show"
Now, this can be enormous fun.

The other name for it is probably social murder, but this is the sort of murder for which you don't get 20 years to life.

First of all you must stand the victim or victims up in uncomfortable or embarrassing circumstances - at dinner at a brightly lit and well known restaurant where your victim has had to book days in advance or possibly at the aisle with his or her mother looking on.

This is frightfully humiliating for the victim. He or she will try to contact you to see where you have got to after waiting for about 20 minutes, so make sure you don't answer the telephone, or have gone out somewhere more exciting. Otherwise you will feel a pang of guilt and the social murder will turn into social suicide.

It is also wise to tell two or three of your acquaintances that this is what you are doing, and why ("He/She is so dull I don't think I could cope with a whole evening") because this will make victim's fate final and decided, and it will destroy any possibility that someone thinks that you made a mistake.

Alternatively, you can always arrange to meet your victim somewhere outside, when it looks as though the heavens will open. Don't show up (but possibly drive past just to have a good look).

You must apologise afterwards, but victim by this time will have got the message and you can continue happily in your normal way of life.

It might be that your victim is persistent in their demands for an apology or explanation. The crushing riposte must then be used without compunction:

"I was kidnapped by aliens and subjected to sexual torture for days on end. Didn't you get my message? They let me out halfway through so I could call your ansaphone"……Might be a little ornate but...

"Sorry - but I just don't like you any more"….

…Is certainly straightforward enough.

Saying NO To Guests

Saying no to guests in the first place is quite easy. Remember you're the boss. An Englishman's home is his castle - or, conversely, it's her alimony. Anyway, the point is, it's your place and you've got the mortgage certificate to prove it.

When saying "NO" in the home, be definite. If it is a spur of the moment "Can I come to dinner?" then the answer can be as simple as "Sorry I am going out".

"There is not enough food/drink in the house" is disastrous. The unwanted guest will offer to bring dinner. It is amazing how people who want to visit take a great deal of persuading that they are not wanted.

The secret-lover-on-leave-for-for-only-one-weekend-before-flying-to-their-doom-over-Bosnia/Iraq/Gatwick might work up to a point, but if your hopeful guest is at all thick skinned he or she might suggest bringing a bottle of champagne and meeting this wonderful lover.

If the excuse was fictitious then you are stumped, if not then you can be quite certain that your thick skinned friend will make a play.

You could always try the health hazard trick: "I must apologise but our septic tank has ruptured" or even "The place is infested with mites. Everything's being fumigated".

It might be a little extreme to paint a cross in red paint on your front door and scrawl underneath it the single word "Plague".

Saying NO To Guests (More Options).

Words along the lines of "We are having a family conference about putting Grandma into a home, but I'll ring you if we get through early", will raise sympathy in your friends and will make sure that you are left well alone. The biggest advantage is, though, that you won't have to make up a result of the meeting.

"Tempers were lost and that is all that I remember. You know what families are like" will work. If it doesn't, make some marks on your legs with red felt-tip to suggest where Granny tried to bite your ankles as you bundled her into the secure van. You may have a problem in the future though, if Granny ever gets to hear about it.

"Sure, I would be delighted to see you; we've got the village fete in the garden on Sunday and the WI will be here making preparations all day Saturday. Shall I put you down for making lemon curd or would you prefer to sort through the jumble for us?" Will stop any casual caller from the city.

"My mother is coming to stay" works wonders on the mother in law and vice versa.

However this does not tend to work on fathers in law. They always tend to fancy the wife of their opposite number. Fathers in law tend to be happy to have their wives accompany them while they drool over said opposite number as well, so you have to make sure that this is addressed to the right person.

To any other type of guest, "My priest" - be non-specific about denomination, though a hint of Holy Roller or Greek Orthodox is a sure hex - "Is coming to stay/ coming to tea / coming to dinner" is a sure fire way of getting some peace and quiet.

A friend of ours was romancing a beautiful girl one summer, but had a suspicion that her interest was less in him than in an invitation to his family's famous house party on the Isle of Wight for Cowes Week.

She rang him one evening to cancel a date, saying that unfortunately her dog was ill and she had to wait in for the vet.

Being naturally suspicious of this story, he phoned her flat an hour later to be told by her flatmate (you can always rely on these people to drop you in it) that she had gone out with another man.

On the Friday before Cowes Week started, he sent her a telegram with this message:

"Cat died STOP Funeral Saturday STOP Family only STOP".

Saying NO To Visits By Friends' Children

Hmmm, awkward. Most friends have an absolute fetish about their mewling, puking infant, however

43

obnoxious. And any slight to the hydrobrachycephalic dwarf in a sailor suit who's just wet themselves on your fine Turkish Kelim is likely to be construed as an insult to your oldest and dearest friend.

The most assured result is to say "Yes" but then to continue the conversation to the point where parents of said kiddy will try to work out a tactful way of saying "Thank you but I've suddenly remembered there's another option. No need to bother you".

Hence - "Of course I will put little Stacey up for the weekend, why, she must be about the same size as Satan, our new Rottweiler".

Or "But she'll have to share a bedroom with Daniel, my forty-five year old uncle who never married. Strange about that. He's so tactile".

Or "What fun she'll have! She can hand round the tray at my local BNP Hell's Angel Affiliate/ Wimmin's Menstrual Finger-Painting Circle [depending on whether you're a man or a woman].

They're awfully sweet people. Misunderstood but sweet".

Watch as brat's parents run a mile.

Saying NO To Relationships

Most people would rather drink cyanide - or Kaliber- than ever arrive at this point. It is infinitely preferable to use any excuse or refuse something else rather than arrive at the hideous embarrassment of looking at the puppy-dog eyes and trembling lower lip of someone who has just offered you their life, their heart and their hand.

"I don't love myself enough to love anyone else", and "My girl/boyfriend wouldn't like it" are really dull, but effective none the less.

"I've only got six months to live", never works, inviting as it does, the response, "Never mind, I'll wait".

"But you give me hives" is particularly offensive. Much better to put someone off you instead. Or say you'll give them an answer at the end of the week and, when the end of the week comes, act as if you've forgotten all about it.

Saying NO to Dinner

You should do this as seldom as possible. Remember there are millions of people starving in China (if you've seen the food there, you won't be surprised - see "NO In The Far East").

There isn't any reason to think that saying yes to dinner means that you are tied in to anything else, and it means that someone else is going to feed you (always say no if you are likely to have to pick up the tab).

However, if is going to be very dull because the company is boring, and the host has bad taste which means that the dinner won't even be a good one, then it is worth refusing. Accept at first and then use one of the stock replies:

"I'm on a sponsored fast for Rwanda [or whichever tiny, enslaved Third World hellhole is currently engaging media sympathy]".

Or: "I'm a bulimic in the downhill stage. I could

come but you'd have to supply me with a large bowl and stand well back".

Or even: "Sorry - but I've got a subsequent engagement". (The invitor will only get this one when they've already put the phone down).

If this is a second invitation to dinner and you not only attended but rather enjoyed the first, and the host in question has exceeding good taste, send a bottle of Knockando single malt whisky by courier to your host's office. If charming and good company is all he is, and he lacks the odd digit in his IQ count, then you may have to cross off the first K. (NO-CAN-DO - geddit?)

Saying NO To A Date

When first dating someone, it is worth deciding from moment one whether or not you would ever sleep with this person (and by "sleep with", we mean, you know, er, actually doing it. As opposed to "go to sleep in front of" i.e. at dinner when they're in the middle of their favourite story of how they're walking all the hills in Scotland over 500 metres and they've only got to the Old Man of Muck or

Scum or Snot or somewhere).

If the answer is no, let not this put you off a free dinner but never forget your own answer.

If the answer is yes perhaps, continue to ask yourself the question, and always be prepared to change your mind. "Not yet" is a very good way of fudging the question, whilst still enjoying the fringe benefits. When it comes to the point, the word is very easy to say - N.O.

Saying NO to Sex

You must have said or implied yes to quite a lot of things to get to this point, and though date rape has become an issue in recent years, it is sensible to avoid getting yourself into a situation you cannot get out of without causing injury to yourself or anger in your opposite number.

The more you drink of an evening, the more tricky this particular question can get.

However, if you find yourself in an unavoidable situation a well-aimed knee in the groin and a quick sprint out of the door tends to work well (but if you still want the meal ticket send flowers the next day with a card saying that you panicked and then never let yourself get in that same situation again).

Saying that you have a dose of the Clap takes a little more nerve, but I would recommend it for those who are less athletic.

Saying NO to Sex with Mike Tyson (A digression)

Speaking of date rape...Do not actually say no to big Mike; on the contrary, accept the invitation for a drink at midnight; laughingly acquiesce to his suggestion of a dalliance in his room at 2.00 am; allow him a lingering kiss; carelessly slip into something loose and then...Call the police.

Even the most prurient of juries will be convinced by your behaviour that you have spent the evening resisting his advances and send him down for five years of rock-cracking, picking oakum or whatever it is that they do in the land of the free.

Oh, and don't forget to hire an agent.

Saying NO Half Way Through

You are now in dangerous water, and the two above have not worked, so a NO has to be sharp and precise.

In the middle of sexual intercourse, the quickest verbal turn off that any of us have experienced is "Is it in?" (for a woman) or "I'm sorry but you remind me so of mummy" (for a man).

Other great NOs halfway through are "You are not going to put that seamy little twig any where near my person" and "What do you mean you haven't got a condom? You'll just have to wrap it up in clingfilm instead" (No it doesn't work - and neither does the cellophane outer-wrapping from a pack of Silk Cut Extra Mild)

"Stay where you are just for a minute. I've got to take out my teeth."

Saying NO afterwards or when it wasn't accepted in the first place

This has to be emphatic, since you haven't been very

successful so far. Comments like "Read my lips" work as do "Have you ever wondered what your nose would look like reconstructed".

Putting terror in the protagonist's heart is simple - "I wonder what your wife/husband/mother/lover/Nigel Dempster would pay me for this story".

Saying NO To Sex With Friends

This is always a little tricky. After all you don't want to lose them as friends, and there is usually some overlaying sexual involvement in friendship between different sexes. You may decide it's not worth saying no. After all weren't you always curious about how they would be in the sack?

The favourite of "We have always been friends and we ought to keep it that way" is a little hackneyed but it does work.

Matching a friend with another is also a good wheeze - "No you would be so perfect for So-and-so. You are made for each other". This takes heat off the moment, and the concentration moves to someone else.

"What a joke" deflates the ego just enough to give you a chance to change the tone of the conversation and if all else fails, try the "What rapture. I've always secretly worshipped you but never dared to speak. Let's get married at once"

Saying NO to Robert Redford

A woman should think about this question very hard. I mean for $1,000,000? If you say no, we are afraid we cannot advise you how.

None of us would.

A man, conversely, doesn't have to think too hard, just say:

"You know I always did think that Butch and Sundance were more than just friends".

Saying NO To Other Indecent Proposals.

If the proposal is not made face to face, then any excuse will do. If made in a restaurant and requiring direct response, on a straw poll we found the ice bucket in the lap trick was one of the most effective. Not only does it cope with the immediate problem, but the other party concerned will have to live with his humiliation when he pays the bill and leaves.

On the other hand, it depends on how indecent the proposal is.

Some sexual proposition will indeed range from the barely imaginable to the scarcely comprehensible, to which a reply might be "Go find a sheep or some other suitable four legged animal".

Others are a good way of wasting an afternoon and clearing your sinuses simultaneously.

Saying NO To Decent Proposals - Saying NO To Marriage

Again, be careful not to upset too many people at the same time, including yourself. It may be worth saying yes until you make up your mind about it. Saying yes keeps the options open, and makes sure that your partner doesn't go off with someone else.

Or you can say, "I need time to think about it, I'll give you an answer at Christmas". This is known as the Bathsheba Everdean Ploy. It is important that, by Christmas, you haven't forgotten the question.

You must realise that the people who get most excited when you are engaged are the parents, and you may find that all the excitement and planning needs to be drawn to a halt sooner rather than later (i.e., when Mummy has mortgaged the house to buy her hat and Daddy is stringing a noose over a beam in the potting shed with the bills spread out on the ground before him).

Then the family will be so pleased that you will find yourself rewarded.

When you finally get around to saying NO (and if you are intending to, don't forget - when you are actually married it isn't a lot of good saying "But I meant to say no"), it is thoughtful to give the guests to your wedding long enough to change their arrangements (unless, of course you have found someone else to marry at the same time), and long enough to recover their wedding presents. Heartbroken as you will be, you certainly won't want the job of packing and posting 350 toasters.

In other words, it is not good form to do it after the priest has said "Do you?" in the face of the assembled congregation.

In this nightmare situation, the only option is to scream: "No, I don't. I am teapot" with a burst of hysterical laughter and then faint.

If you think that you might be approaching this kind of scenario, have one of your friends, wearing pince-nez and a Van Dyck beard in reserve at the back of the church.

As you hit the floor, he must be walking forward shouting: "Ach. What a great pity. Another relapse and after so many months of treatment. Never mind, better get her/him back to Rampton as quickly as possible. Taxi!".

And you'd better pray there's a black cab within hailing distance because people can be terribly unkind to the mentally troubled.

And the things they'll be throwing as you retreat through the church doors will be a lot heavier than confetti.

Saying NO To Marriage (At A Distance).

There are various ways of doing it, but the best that I've heard of was a girl who wrote her fiance a letter saying that before she married she felt that she had to find herself and her god.

She didn't think it proper to be married in church without being sure she believed in God, and she couldn't get married in a registry office because she didn't know whether she should be married in church. She said she was going to travel around the Far East soaking up their religions, to see what really matched her aura. Her fiance thought her so weird that he bore the burden of guilt and broke their engagement, much to her satisfaction.

This, however, is not something that you can try on anyone who knows you very very well unless you spend some time leading up to it.

Otherwise your partner will know for sure what you are up to, and the guilt will fall on you.

Another sure fire way of getting out of the ultimate

engagement is to go off to get a tan before the wedding. Book two weeks in advance (and preferably get the loved one to pay) at a decent hotel on a remotish island - Barbados is a bit too cosmopolitan- and check out the local talent.

After getting settled in, cable your ex-beloved and tell him/her to start sending the wedding presents back because he/she will be at the altar on his/her own.

This will upset said ex-beloved somewhat and it may be worth going into hiding for a while afterwards.

The simplest but least thoughtful way of cancelling an engagement is to engineer a whopping great row and send the ring/car keys/house keys back by registered mail in the morning (or demand that they should be sent to you). The price of this (depending on the size of the rock etc.) is a tenner at the most, and you are able to claim to be the injured party. But you will have lost the ring, and the use of the car.

The best way of compensating for this is the overspending on the joint credit card the day before.

Saying NO With Flowers

This takes a little bit of thought and is best suited to the spring and summer months, though any decent florist can come up with a Marguerite daisy if you can't pick one off somebody's lawn.

Take your daisy, pull all the petals out bar one and send it through to your ex with a note saying that it will never work out. The other party will never be quite sure who does not love whom, but will be too afraid to ask. It may be best to press the flower first if you have any distance that you have to send it, because otherwise it might have rotted by the time it arrives.

The arrival of a mouldy and mutilated bit of vegetation might lose its romantic significance.

(This trick can also be attempted using a dead tarantula with all its legs pulled off. Be warned; if the recipient is particularly dense they might think it's a chocolate truffle surrounded by eight Twiglets and scoff the lot).

A perecipient never actually planted them in the first place!

Saying NO To Presents

This can be very hard indeed to carry out successfully. The end result should be that you are able to accept the offering if you wish, but with no other strings attached. "I simply cannot accept" is the best recognised, but with something so definitive as that, you lose your ability to bargain.

"Did you keep the receipt?" might be the best response..

Saying NO To Flowers

Both men and women send flowers either as a greeting, an apology or as a thank you. You should never feel under pressure to send flowers back (besides, this may cost money, and, anyway, if flowers are sent the sender will only know from the receiver whether they reached their destination or not).

Flowers are extremely pleasant to receive and the only good reason for turning them down is if you are allergic to them, and even then you can give them to next door's dog to eat.

You can always deny that you received them, or say that there was a very silly message on them and you couldn't read the signature (a great put down to the person who sent them).

Flowers, like so many other things are part of the "Don't say no yet" scenario.

Saying NO to...The Fur Coat

Many would consider this deeply distasteful. If you fall into this category, but are interested in the concept of being given exceptionally expensive presents, then you must be very careful about your reply.

"Darling, don't you care about me at all? Someone may attack me in the street and it would all be your fault" is not likely to have the desired effect.

You will probably be given a personal alarm to slip in your knickers. Or a large Korean bodyguard (though it's unlikely you could fit all of him into your knickers as well, but it might be fun if you could).

The result that you want is to turn the coat into something that you would actually like to receive, whilst at the same time telling your benefactor where he went wrong.

Much better is the reply "Darling, I'm so sorry but I only wear ermine".

If he is then stupid enough to try to buy you an ermine coat I am afraid it is time for the bottle of Knockando (see dinner).

If he isn't, it should result in a nice Loewe or Versace suit instead.

Saying NO to... The Chanel Suit/ Gieves & Hawkes Suit

However much you always wanted a Chanel suit you must turn it down. Men have no taste when it comes to buying them, and they tend to buy the classic which manages to make even the most nubile young lady look in her mid forties.

Sulk, pout but don't utter the N word until he asks you what's wrong and then tell him it isn't going to look good on you, or that you don't feel comfortable.

You can always exchange it (unless he bought it really cheap in which case he isn't worth the trouble).

Women have the same trouble. They all imagine that all men look good in the lumpy undertaker's mute garb perfected by Savile Row but invented by Gieves & Hawkes. Start wearing it for all occasions - not just to the office but around the home, on weekends in the country and trips to the beach. She'll soon get sick of the sight of it and the Oxfam Shop will be so grateful.

Saying NO to ..... the Lambourghini

Say something like "Thank you so much. I've always wanted a little car. Will you give me driving lessons?" This should freak the donor out so much that you will probably end up with BSM lessons instead.

Boys to say NO to.

Quentin, Jerry, Gavin, Rodrique and Torquill;

Spanish boys over the age of 14 unless he's a gypsy

(actually to stay in terms of legality you should say no to Spanish boys under the age of 14 too);

Spanish men over the age of 14 (Not a legal issue but a question of taste - have you ever tasted a Spanish moustache with its indefinable essence of stale olive oil and Southern European industrial-strength cologne?);

Men with flared wheel arches;

Men with flares, rugs attached to their fronts (or backs) and medallion men;

Cabinet Ministers strongly into Law and Order;

Circus midgets;

Men with Penile Extensions (they still have Little Willie

Syndrome);

Serial killers on Death Row;

Those who look like Jim Davidson;

Those who sound like Jim Davidson;

Those who behave like Jim Davidson;

Jim Davidson;

Men who break wind in bed and then say; "Whew! Better out than in, eh?";

Men who burst into tears when Gazza strains his groin but don't bat an eyelid when you don't get that promotion after three years' hard work;

Men who come to soon and then don't stick around.

Girls to say NO to.

Tracy, Sharon and any Essex girl;

Any gutsy, luvable, full of folk wisdom heroine of a Carla Lane sitcom;

Girls with shaven heads, rings through nostril and bricklayer' dungarees;

Girls with large and uncomprehending husbands;

Girls who sniff;

Welsh girls - the sing song, "Hello campers" voice can grind you down more easily that two tonnes of nutty slack on your head;

Anybody you work with (but we all know that we

can get around this one with a little effort);

Anybody with bad teeth;

Girls who don't come at all and then stick around forever.

Saying NO To A Toyboy

It is worth testing the mettle of a toyboy before you decide to say no. There are some that need no teaching, but according to a recent survey done on monkeys, good sex is not an intuitive act, but is more of a skill to be learnt and understood (if you must know, they separated monkeys by sex until they were adults and then compared their pattern of sexual behaviour when the different sexes were mixed)

If you have a good toyboy, keep him for as long as you possibly can, he's worth his weight in gold.

Do remember though that you might lack in conversation, and if you will excuse the pun, successful toyboys tend to be a little cocky.

If you don't mind shocking the chap a little bit there are some great ways of saying no.

Being the senior in the relationship, the no should always carry a gem of advice.

"Get a life" isn't really very kind, nor is "Go find someone your own age to play with".

A friend once told her young man that it would never work until he understood women a little better. The only suggestion that she could give him was to go and sleep with a man so that he would know how it felt!.

Saying NO To The Female Equivalent

The female equivalent of a toyboy is a bimbo. Never say no (as long as you can afford it).

AND SAYING NO IN GENERAL

Saying NO In Business

With a little practice this comes naturally.

If anyone rings up trying to sell you advertising, a little experience will teach you the tone of voice within two sentences.

The most effective reply is that you have run out of budget or you didn't have any in the first place. They will then tell you that you ought to find some budget and the perfect answer to this is that it will have to come out of your own salary.

Nobody gets paid enough not to respect this answer.

Cold callers will then disappear.

If the call is not cold then you only have yourself to

blame anyway. If someone tries to sell you something, you say no, and then they push for time to visit your office, you have no alternative but to be out when they call.

It may be cruel but that is the only way of getting through to some salesmen who are flogging you something deeply distasteful. They are truly thick skinned so there is no need to worry about hurting their feelings.

Sometimes you need to be cruel to be kind (or that's what our parents told us anyway). If however, they get through this one too, listen to them patiently. Their sales pitch only ever lasts about 10 minutes until they pause for a response.

Do not encourage them.

Be polite, say that it was interesting, show them the door, and think up a request for a suitably impossible piece of data without which you would never dream of purchasing ("Can you tell me the exact percentage of commuters rather than tourists on the same day of each month going through a particular tube station?")

Saying No to The Free Lunch

Who says that there is no such thing as a free lunch?

You can always say no later. Never be bamboozled by other people's expense accounts.

It is certainly easier to say no to someone who invites you to tea to discuss a matter, than to someone who invites you to the Opera with dinner somewhere fabulous afterwards, but never let your conscience ruin the evening.

NO goes terribly well into a thank you letter - In the former case, a little irony comes in useful:

Mr Sidney Toasties
Dundunkin
Oolong Avenue
Peckham

Dear Mr Toasties

Thank you for your unbounded generosity in the matter of tea yesterday.

After reflecting on the matter over a stiff drink later I fear that it is unlikely that we will every see eye to eye on the basic matters of life.
However, we should remain friends, and I will reciprocate the invitation.
Meanwhile, please find enclosed a packet of Earl Grey tea which I highly recommend above Ty-phoo.

Yours

In the case of the latter, the reply should be more generous

Emmanuel Crush-Bar Esq
Plutochracy Manor
Wheneverfield
Surrey

Dear Mr Crush Bar,

Thank you for your unbounded generosity in a glorious evening last night.
Unfortunately, I fear that I cannot continue in business with you, because I can see where a large proportion of the

marketing/ sales budget goes.
However, I would be delighted if you would try to persuade me again.

Yours sincerely.

Saying NO To More Work

This is essential to anyone who works in any sort of office environment, but has to be very carefully done so as to enhance you reputation for hard work rather than to diminish it.

You must never say no, but rather not yet.

"Yes of course I'll do it for you, but I can't until the middle of next week. I absolutely have to leave the office by 8 for the next three days" works a dream. You will get away with not having to do anything, and probably a pay rise as well.

Saying NO to Customers

In any business we are told that the customer is always right. Well he is not, and anyone who has ever had customers of any sort knows this.

A large degree of tact, give and take and good manners will solve nearly every problem, but there are some people who will never be satisfied.

The simple answer is to stop supplying them and put a writ out for the money that they owe.

Saying NO to an Official Engagement.

The art of this is delegation. Get someone else to do it on your behalf, because no-one kills the messenger these days (and seeing the quality of most motorcycle despatch riders who call sweatily at our doors, more's the pity).

Saying NO On Behalf of a Colleague.

Don't hesitate. Drop them in it. They'd do the same for you.

"Sorry - he's off water-skiing".

"Actually, he thinks your idea has about as much merit as concrete suppositories. But he says, don't give up. Keep plugging'.

"He's on the ledge of the 14th Floor. He'll be down

in a moment".

Or the best yet:

"He told me to fob you off with a polite excuse but I can't think of one".

Saying NO to Door to Door Salesmen

For anyone old or infirm, shy or worried about being interrupted whilst doing something much more entertaining during the day, there are stickers that you can get saying that you're not interested in buying anything from door to door salesmen, and that they should please go away.

Unfortunately, the inference drawn from one of these by any salesman worth his salt is that you are so susceptible to the old patter that you dare not let him over the threshold. He will therefore attempt to get in under any number of guises from a missionary nun to the solicitor and executor of a long lost relative's will which may very easily name you as chief beneficiary.

No, much the best way of deterring these people is

to play a recording of a damned great Doberman barking its guts out every time the doorbell rings. Or listen to his pitch, feign delight and amazement, sign all the sales forms and the cheque and send him on his way rejoicing.

Always use the name Hermann Munster when signing these things.

Saying NO to Double Glazing Salesmen

Invite them in. Ask them to spread out their samples on the table. Listen while they describe the tensile strength of the samples. Get a hammer. Break the samples.

Saying NO to Jehovah's Witnesses

They ring the doorbell.

You say, through the closed door: "Yes who is it?"

They answer - through closed door - :"We are Jehovah's Witnesses. Did you know that the Lord God of Hosts will be born again?".

You open the door dressed in bath-towel, false beard and sandals and say: "You're doing good work lads. Pass on the message but don't give out my address".

Then slam the door.

Saying NO To Beggars.

Very simple. You're gambit begins with the words: "Do you have change for a five pound note?".

If they say yes, you respond: "Then lend us two quid till Tuesday".

If they say no, you respond: "Neither do I. Wish I had one".

Of course, nowadays the beggar may be masquerading as a news vendor, selling copies of The BiIssue. There are several ways of dealing with this type of mendicant. You can always carry a copy of the paper, but that probably means you have had to buy one from someone else; you could adopt the Biblical technique of avoiding his eye and crossing road or you can point out to him that if he takes the insulting and anti-establishment rag apart page by page, he should be able to fashion for himself a rude hut, thereby solving the problem of his homelessness.

Saying NO to Oprah Winfrey

This is quite easy but requires observation. When approached by the Queen of American soul-bearing to appear on her ghastly show, either say "Bugger off, Fatty" or "Bugger off, Skinny" depending which chair in her feeding/dieting swing-cycle she happens to be occupying at the time.

Saying NO to Michael Aspel

You don't want to go on This Is Your Life and have to pretend that you liked your old school headmaster or that Michael Caine is a bosom buddy. Pretend that the presenter's puerile disguise is so effective that you don't recognise him, jump into your car and roar off. Alternatively, every time he asks "Do you recognise this voice" look blank and say "No".

Saying NO to the Police.

Don't say no. Say nothing. And say it in the presence of your solicitor. Why should they need you to help them with their enquiries? God knows, there's enough of them.

Saying NO in Court

Whether you have or haven't done what you have been charged with, always plead not guilty.

And then elaborate. "It wasn't me. I wasn't there. It was my twin brother - one's good, the other's evil, I'm the good one. The voices told me to do it. I was in Hawaii. I was watching television. Those aren't my finger prints. I never laid a hand on her. She was asking for it. I don't recognise this court. I've been stitched up. Where am I? I've just woken up. It was the PMT. I've got Alzheimers...".

You never know, you may get away with it. Ernest Saunders did. But don't, whatever you do, try it in your jokey Irish accent.

Saying NO to Children.

Let a surreptitious clip round the ear-hole do your talking for you. It's the only language they understand. If the child's parent hoves into view to find out while their babe is bawling his eyes out say, solicitously: "Did 'oo fall over, Kevin? Let me kiss it better". It's their word against yours.

Saying NO in tricky situations

Let's cut to the chase. Saying No isn't so hard when you're in command of events - when you're at the wheel of your Ferrari Testarossa with your foot down or when Cilla has just handed you your Littlewoods cheque for a cool million or when your loved one has one of his tantrums about dinner being late and you've got Warren Beatty stashed in the bedroom closet desperately trying to do his flies up.

But what about those tricky situations?

You know what I mean. When all eyes are on you and your bowels have turned to water, your hair is standing on end, your hands are trembling like a tuning-fork and you've been caught with your trousers down (or your skirts up) and nothing in the world can save you.

How do you say no then?

Read on...

Saying No When Caught In A Compromising Position With A Person Not Your Spouse

By a compromising position we do not mean a touch of lipstick on the collar or a jock-strap mysteriously found in the connubial duvet - we mean bedroom joy-riding with the roof down, the gearstick stuck in fifth gear, the smell of burning rubber in the air and the meter well into the red - and suddenly you hear sirens. IE. you have been taken in flagrante delicto.

Picture the scene. You've taken the day off work. You've hustled the Mexican plumber or Italian circus contortionist of your dreams through the front door with a furtive glance over your shoulder to make sure the neighbours aren't peeking. You snatch a furtive lunch in the living room (half a glass of luke-warm champagne to wash down the handful of Pro Plus pills) and then, shedding clothes at every step, you rush them into the bedroom. All right, halfway through a game in which one of you is Spartacus and the other is Emperor's Daughter Taken Hostage, the door opens and in walks your spouse. It doesn't matter why they're back - a rail strike, a meteor striking the office, a disembodied voice whispering in their ear "Return hooome! Return hooome!" - all that matters is that they're standing in the doorway, their eyes are bulging like a diver's with the bends and their jaw just bouncing down the stairs to the basement.

You will then hear those words which, for so many, are the beginning of the end of the known world: "What is the meaning of this? Are you having an affair?".

The simple and only solution is to say "No". And keep saying it.

But don't say it in a half-hearted, giggly way as you try and hide your shame-faced expression behind your lover's hairy arse. This is fatal. The "It-Was-Only-Horseplay-That-Got-Out-Of-Hand-Can't-You-Take-A-Joke?' defence is weak at the best of times and passes back control of events to the person on whom the "joke" is being played. And since this person - humiliated, hurt and with steam coming out of their ears as if from a high pressure boiler

- is unlikely to see the funny side, your gentle lob will be returned over the net with a forehand smash that will lift you off your feet and leave you in the Duchess of Kent's lap somewhere in the VIP Seats. As many an MP caught loitering in a public lavatory has found out, the "high jinks" approach to sexual malpractice falls to pieces under the withering stare of the magistrate.

No, take control. Simply deny everything - even the evidence of your spouse's own eyes. The moment you have been discovered, both you lover and you should get off the bed and, calmly and carefully put on your clothes. Make the bed. Open the window. Whatever happens, keep moving - not with desperate, fumble-fingered haste but with deliberate speed. Your lover should be slipping out of the room (and the house) just as you are smoothing out the counterpane. At no point in this process, should you or your piece of totty meet your spouse's eye. This will break the spell.

Instead, what you must be doing is batting away the stream of questions from your spouse: "What the hell do you think you're doing? Don't I mean anything to you anymore? How could you do this in our own bedroom? Doesn't trust mean anything to you?....." and so on.

Deny everything. Not just the affair but reality itself. "I don't know what you're talking about", "What do you mean?", "Nothing's going on".

Faced with this blank stonewalling, the aggrieved party will pick up an offending panty or a condom as damning evidence - "And what do you call this, then?". You reply: "What precisely do you mean? Is it one of yours?". This will lead to a further torrent of hysterical questioning but just keep your head down and keep answering their questions with questions of your own. "I don't understand you. What are you trying to say?"., "What 'intolerable situation' are we talking about?", "Which 'piece of vacuous blonde fluff' are you referring to?".

Try and develop an expression of amused bafflement mixed with sweet reason on your face - a difficult attitude to maintain but will help you achieve the desired result: that of making your partner question their own sanity.

After about fifteen minutes of this, your spouse will be beginning to flag. By now you should be downstairs sitting in an armchair leafing nonchalantly through the Daily Telegraph (a good thick paper which offers a modicum of body armour in case your spouse decides to back up their barrage of questions with a saucepan). By now, they will be beginning to hesitate and change their tack: it won't be the fact that you've been caught riding bareback on the familial Sely Posturepedic that is amazing them but you attitude. "How can you behave like this?", "Like what, dear?", "Like that. Just sitting there, reading, as if nothing has happened?", "Why shouldn't I?"

And, after a while, your spouse will begin to question, not you (because that's not going anywhere), but there own sanity. Did I really find them in bed together? Yes, but, if I did, where's the other person? (In the back of a minicab, trying to wiggle back into a pair of drainpipe jeans while they speed ever further away from the scene of the crime). The bedroom! That's it, there must be some evidence there (But no. The bed is made. The window is open. The scent of roses from the garden).

Slowly but surely, the thought forms in your partner's mind: "Did I... did I... *imagine* it all?"

And then the game is won (True, you will catch a baffled and suspicious look on your spouse's face over the next couple of days. Ignore it. Don't overplay your hand by humming the theme tune of "The Twilight Zone" under your breath).

Saying No When Challenged To A Duel

Outside a few rarefied environments (the foothills of the Pathan Himalayas, "Newsnight" interviews with Jeremy Paxman on, the poolside of all-female health club The Sanctuary in Covent Garden"), you are unlikely to find yourself challenged to a duel to the death, especially a trifle (though criticising any dessert served at The Restaurant in London's Hyde Park Hotel is likely to provoke a visit to your table from Marco Pierre White, which, if you've seen the size of him, you'll know is not dissimilar to mortal combat).

On the other hand, stranger things have happened

(who'd have thought that Jimmy Tarbuck would ever get another series on national television after "Winner Takes All"?).

You might be walking down the Mall, taking the air, when you receive a sharp shove in the back. You turn to face the offender and find your face stinging from the slap of a kid glove and the fateful words:

"You have besmirched a lady's name/cheated at cards/parked in a disabled zone. I challenge you to a duel. Do you accept?"

If there are no witnesses, your course of action is clear. Push the bastard in front of a taxi (the Mall is full of them) and make for the horizon at Mach 1.

But there are always witnesses, dammit. Your girlfriend, your colleagues, your bank manager, your mates from school, a documentary team from Channel 4, rich and influential people you've been trying to get on the phone for months... they all suddenly appear at your elbow, looking at you with a fascinated and admiring air of expectation. Don't these busy-bodies know that by dawn next day, you are likely to be filled so full of holes that your resemblance to a Swiss Cheese will for once extend beyond your overpowering bodily odour?

Under these circumstances, you can't say No. It's just not possible. Could you really live under the shame and ignominy of everyone knowing that you have a larger interior yellow streak than a Walls Lemon Mivvy? (The worst of it is the only people who'll ever sleep with you again will do it out of a sense of pity - knowledge of which is the most effective way of ensuring poor sexual performance other than thinking about John Selwyn Gummer in the nude).

You have to accept. But once you have, the advantage is yours. You see, if you are the recipient of a challenge, the choice of weapons and location is yours.

"Soft pillows in zero gravity" will soon clear up the matter with honour satisfied (though you should specify man-made fibres for the pillow stuffing if you suffer a serious allergy to feathers. After all, don't want a chance of hurting ourselves, do we?, even if the most mortal wound you are likely to suffer in the encounter is a bad case of the sniffles).

The modern equivalent of the duel is much more common and much more dangerous - the pub challenge.

"Oi, you, ponce! Did you spill my pint?" is how it begins. "Outside, now!".

Console yourself that, even these modern times, the code of chivalry still lives. As the Neanderthal with the shaved head and union jack T-shirt, turns to receive the baying applause of his mates and make for the door, remember that the choice of weapons is yours. And your choice of weapons should be the nearest bar-stool planted in the nape of his thick neck while his back is still turned. And who says that honour is dead?

Saying No When Found In Your Loved One's Underwear

In some households, it's not who wears the trousers that counts but who wears the panties.

How many are there, we wonder, where, upstairs, the husband is prancing up and down in front of the mirrored wardrobe, holding the skirts of his wife's Balenciaga just above the thigh so he can glimpse the stockings underneath while downstairs, in the garage, his wife is fitting on her B&Q hubby's tool-belt and enjoying the cool, strong, strangely exciting feel of the leather as she straps it round her waist?

Who knows and, indeed, who cares? This kind of lip-smacking speculation about suburban perversion is unhealthy and should be kept where it safely belongs, in the pages of the mass circulation Sunday papers.

However if cross-dressing is your particular - how shall we put this? - bent, then be prepared for that moment when the bedroom door opens unexpectedly and you discovered dolled up as if an extra from "Four Weddings And A Funeral" - but as a bridesmaid as opposed to the groom.

You then hear the shocked question: "Darling? Are you, er, you know, a transvestite?".

If you are a woman, how to say no is not much of a

problem. Just turn and face the bewildered man and plant a strange, yearning kiss on his open mouth and then drag him over to the bed, explaining that it's always been a secret desire of yours to play the dominant role. Men love to uncork a hidden stream of wantonness surging through their women. It makes them think that, after all, you may not be as hard to turn on as an Austin Maxi on a winter's morning (since so many women lose interest in sex after marriage - ie. like on about Day 3).

If you are a man, no excuse is going to work. Just brazen it out. As you stand there in your organdie and tulle, say brightly: "Darling, you'll never guess who just called? John Major. He wants me to take up a senior position in the Cabinet". This will explain everything. Just make sure that, in the future, you don't give yourself a larger dress allowance than she gets.

If you are discovered not by a forgiving loved one in the bedroom but a Sergeant of the Metropolitan Police in a public lavatory, the only thing to do is give him a large and lubricious wink. Who knows?, he might be wearing a Baby Doll teddy and suspenders underneath that cruel blue serge.

Saying No When Discovered With A Smoking Gun

Isn't it always the way? You plan the perfect crime, you establish the cast-iron alibi, you strew a trail of red herrings, you cast suspicion onto innocent parties, and yet having just pumped some worthless rat full of lead in the library, you look up, gun in hand, to find Marmaduke, Lord Merridew peering down at you quizzically through his trademark monocle while Inspector Glumm of the Barsetshire Constabulary reaches for the derbies.

You hear the words: "Excuse me, Madame, am I to understand that you have just murdered Jasper the blackmailing cousin in order to cover up that it was you who stole the family pearls some twenty long summers ago?".

Well, this is pretty bloody obvious isn't it since Jasper is still twitching on the fine Aubusson doing his impersonation of a kitchen colander what with all the perforations you have just made in him? That, and the fact, that you have a 9mmm Parbellum

Mauser still smoking in your hands.

Do not dignify the question with an answer. Point the gun at Marmaduke and the Inspector and just hope you've got enough bullets left over from Jasper to finish off the job.

Naturally, a "smoking gun" can mean a number of other damaging items just as incriminating as your actual smoking gun. It might be anything from a pie stolen from the kitchen in the middle of the night when you and your partner are on a strict diet all the way up to a secret document with your signature on it authorising the export of super guns to the Iraqis. The point about damaging items is that they damage. So use them to cause as much damage as possible and hope you can escape in the mayhem. If you are caught at three o'clock in the morning with a steak and kidney pie halfway to your lips, shove it in your loved one's face - or, if Lord Justice Scott won't change his line of questioning in open session about a particularly embarrassing piece of evidential documentation, pick it up and scream hysterically "Lady Thatcher made me do it. That's right. The old milksnatcher herself". In either case, your life is over but what a way to go.

Saying No To Giving Up Your Place In The Lifeboat

Just after midnight, the luxury cruiser hits an iceberg and is holed beneath the waterline. As the First Class promenade deck attains the sloping angle of Mont Blanc, it becomes clear that, due to an oversight of the designers, there are just not enough lifeboats to go around. By dint of judicious gouging and scratching, you manage to clamber through the screaming mob of steerage passengers and into the last crowded boat just as it is about to be lowered into the brine. You sit back comfortably anticipating a peaceful two or three hours bobbing up and down exposed to the healthful ozone before being picked up by the US 3rd Fleet. Then some blue-eyed, golden haired moppet of sixteen puts her interfering head over the gunwales and begs: "Oh, won't any of you kind people give me your seat? I am too young to die in the frozen deep". And, of a sudden, all eyes are on you.

If you are a woman, the answer comes naturally: "No. Naff off" and no one will think any the worse of you. (Women can get away with anything in matters of sentiment. If a man had beaten loveable, plucky, credit-to-the-game Martina Navratilova in her last Wimbledon Finals instead of Conchita Martinez, the crowd would have torn him limb from limb. That being said, if Martina had been playing against a man, she'd have beaten him anyway).

If you are a man, then a little pre-preparation is in order. You must rise slowly from your seat: "Excuse me, miss. I am Dr. Heinrich Schlitz of the Mount Zion Hospital, California (or any other name suggesting medical probity). I would willingly give you my seat but...." At this point you lift up your hand so that everyone can see that you are holding a small black bag. "...There is a little boy waiting in my hospital, waiting for what's inside this bag, waiting for the heart that will bring him back to life. He needs this heart so that he can roam once more the green fields of his homeland and if I could get out of the boat and leave the bag I surely would..." At this point shake the bag a bit so that the passengers can see that it's securely linked to your wrist by what seems to be a security handcuff (in actual fact, a bicycle chain or whatever's nearest to hand as you rummage through your cabin)"....But I can't". By this time the other passengers will image that they can hear the sobbing of violins and, however much the moppet screams, "Open the bag, ya chiseler", she'll never get your place. Possibly the other passengers might be so moved that they might prise the moppet's grasping fingers away from the rails with boathooks, a truly satisfying sight - and even more satisfying will be the knowledge that the black bag is actually filled with the jewels and large denomination bonds that you coolly rifled from the cabins of your fellow passengers while they were panicking like headless chickens after the first impact.

A word of warning though. If the US Fleet doesn't pick you up after the first day (and a small lifeboat is an awfully easy thing to miss on a radar screen) then there's going to come a time when your lifeboat's members start to draw lots to see who gets eaten first. And if they find out that your black bag doesn't carry salvation for little Harry Traub of Barbedwireville, N. Dakota but inedible jewellery, you are likely to be first on the menu - even before the ship's biscuits run out.

Saying No To The Mafia When Asked To Repay A Loan

When the man with the cauliflower ear and the squashed nose appears on your doorstep to enquire about the little matter of £50,000 outstanding, the only thing you can do is sell one of your kidneys.

Saying No To Your Bank Manager When Asked To Repay A Loan.

Sell one of his kidneys.

Saying No When Asked For A Dance By A Lonely, Fat Person.

You can't say no. How can you refuse those large, brimming cow-like eyes. It would be like shooting Bambi and selling the carcass to Bernard Matthews. You must accept.

But make sure, as you lead the perspiring lardass out onto the floor, like a tugboat shifting an oil-tanker to open water, that you have a notice pinned to your back on which is written in fluorescent felt-tip highlighter: "I Am Only Doing This Out Of Pity".

Saying NO To A Drink

Pressure of time is useful, "I have to be somewhere else in fifteen minutes", but that fifteen minutes is extraordinarily expandible.

"I am driving" makes you out to be a party pooper and after a while, is it is any sort of size of gathering you will feel like a social leper.

Instead say "Yes - if it's vintage Krug".

Alas, it never is.

The Ultimate NO Gesture.

A gift of this book with its many many ways of saying no will make your position more than adequately clear.

One last comment - as the slope said the perpendicular "I decline"